Animal Attack

Greg Pyers

sundance

Published by Sundance Publishing
P.O. Box 1326, 234 Taylor Street, Littleton, MA 01460

Copyright © text Greg Pyers

First published 1999 as Phenomena by
Horwitz Martin
A Division of Horwitz Publications Pty Ltd
55 Chandos St., St. Leonards NSW 2065 Australia

Exclusive United States Distribution: Sundance Publishing

ISBN 0-7608-4947-1

Printed in Canada

Contents

Author's Note

The different ways people relate to animals fascinate me. I have worked in a zoo for many years. I know that most people like bears but don't like snakes. Why this is so I can only guess. Whatever the reason, it only matters to me that people understand an animal.

All animals are alike in that they have four basic needs—food, water, oxygen, and shelter. A snake has venom to help it kill its prey, not to attack people. If a shark eats a swimmer, it is not an evil animal. It is simply hungry.

I believe that when we understand these things, we can learn ways of living together with animals.

Greg Pyers believes there is much we can do for animals, including creating habitats for wild creatures in our own backyards. And he practices what he preaches. When he is not creating habitats for animals, Greg writes about animals. He has published more than thirty books.

Introduction

Have you seen the label on cans of tuna that says "Dolphin Safe"? That means that when the fish were caught, no dolphins were harmed. It also means that people think dolphins are more important than tuna. Imagine the words "Tuna Safe" on a can of dolphin meat!

You might say that a tuna is "just a fish," but a dolphin is "completely different." There are, after all, places where people can actually see and touch wild dolphins. There are other places, though, where dolphins are killed to protect fishing grounds.

How people relate to animals is not always easy to explain. We share the world with more than a million species of animals. In our daily lives we come in contact with just some of these species. Some are animals we keep as pets, animals we eat, and animals we watch in the zoo or the circus. Some animals cause disease. Some attack us. We read about animals in books and see them on TV. Wild animals live in our neighborhoods, and tiny animals crawl around our houses.

This book explores the amazing ways people think about and relate to animals. It looks at how people treat animals and the ways that animals affect people.

How do animals affect your life?

Chapter 1: Introduction

Imagine . . .

your home has been invaded by creatures that look like they came from outer space.

JOEL CARO WAS VERY TIRED. He had just vacuumed the entire house. Vacuuming is not something many 11-year-olds like doing once, let alone three times in the same week.

His mother was angry, not with Joel, but with the chicken farm next door. Three times that week, clouds of dust had blown from the farm over the Caro house. Every room had been filled with a dusty haze. A coating of powder was on the carpets and furniture. Mrs. Caro had had enough. While Joel cleaned up the mess, she went into town to complain to the town council.

"Heaven knows what's in that dust," Mrs. Caro had protested.

"They put chemicals in the food so the chickens grow bigger, don't they?" she asked.

Joel was sitting on the couch in the living room, reading. The morning was warm. He had just showered after his housecleaning. His mother would probably be in town for a few more hours, he thought.

A gentle tugging at his pant leg caused Joel to smile as he read. "Good boy, Toby," he said. Toby was Joel's new puppy. Joel loved the little dog. He liked its playful attention.

The gentle tugging became rough tugging.

"Gee, go easy, boy." Joel looked up from his book to discipline the dog. There was no dog! Something else was tugging at his pants!

He screamed. "What is that? Mom!"

Joel was frightened. He kicked his leg, sending the creature tumbling across the carpet. Its legs were waving in the air, like a beetle's legs, only it wasn't a beetle. And it wasn't the only one. Joel looked around the room. They were everywhere, over a hundred of them. They were as big as soccer balls.

Joel quickly tucked his legs under him. There was safety on the couch.

"What are they?"

Horrified, Joel sat stiffly on his couch and watched the creatures. They didn't seem to have a head. They only had jaws opening and closing as their legs and their feelers waved.

They appeared to be chewing at nothing in particular. Still, they were leaving piles of droppings as they inched their fat, brown bodies around the room. They were disgusting.

"I need to get out of here," Joel whispered to himself. His eyes were wide with fear.

His heart was racing.

Then he heard something—a yelp.

"Toby!"

The puppy's call came from the hallway.

"I'm coming, boy."

Joel planned his route through the alien creatures. He remembered a movie he'd seen where the hero escaped from crocodiles by using their heads as stepping stones. Joel thought he was even worse off. At least in the movie the hero knew what he was up against.

On the count of three, Joel set off. Four steps into his run, his left foot came down on one of the creatures. Its body cracked like an egg. Squished guts oozed over Joel's shoes.

Joel had almost reached the hall door when his path was blocked by a silver-plated insect. It was the size of a bulldog. It waved its head and feelers at Joel like it was sniffing out a meal.

It may have been Joel's yelling or arm waving that did it. The monster silverfish turned and ran into the kitchen.

"Toby!" Joel ran for the door and flung it open. He saw what looked like crows pecking at the puppy's lifeless body. Only these crows didn't fly away. They jumped, like fleas.

This was all too much for Joel. He made a dash for the front door. But blocking his way was a shiny thread. Joel ran into the thread and found that it was so sticky that he couldn't get loose.

Then he noticed the great hairy legs coming toward him. . . .

Chapter 1
Animals in the House

Like it or not, your house is a habitat, a home, for animals. Not just for the spider you might see near the ceiling, but for dozens of animal species.

Skin Eaters

The story of Joel and Toby may be far-fetched. But millions of tiny creatures like those in the story live in your house. The soccer-ball creatures are dust mites. These microscopic animals eat dead skin. Humans provide the mites with a constant supply of food.

Human skin is shed, not like snake skin in one piece, but in tiny flakes. The flakes fall off every time we get dressed or scratch an itch. The flakes snow down on the dust mites living in the carpet or in a mattress. In fact, there may be 500 dust mites per gram of mattress dust.

Your Home Is Their Home

It is hardly surprising that a house should be home for all kinds of animal life. All animals need food, shelter, and water. There's a huge supply of all three in any house.

There are many different habitats in a house. Each habitat is right for a different species. Carpet to a dust mite is like a pond to a duck. Let's look at what else lives in house habitats.

Another Mattress Dweller

A bedbug drinks blood. It sticks a blood vessel with its beaklike mouth and draws the blood into its gut. The bedbug injects an anticoagulant—a chemical—into the blood vessel. This chemical stops clotting and often causes itching and swelling. Of course, the best time for a bedbug to feed is when the host animal is sound asleep. Then blood sucking won't be interrupted.

A sleeping human body must be delicious to a bedbug. It's an easy meal, too. All that blood arrives at the same place and same time every night.

host: Body on which another animal lives or feeds.

15

Adult bedbugs are about one-quarter inch long, brown, and wingless. When their human host is away, perhaps scratching a few bites, the bedbugs hide close to their feeding ground. This could be a crack in the wall. It could be among the blankets or in the mattress.

Each female bedbug finds a crack, maybe on the bed frame, where she lays up to 50 eggs. New bedbugs hatch from the eggs a week or two later.

Bedbugs are tough insects. Even if the human hosts go on vacation, the insects can survive. Bedbugs can live for up to five months without a meal of blood. Some bedbugs may even hitch a ride on their hosts. Then they move into the guest room or sleeping bag to find a new host.

In Darkest Crannies

Kitchens are like rain forests. Many kinds of animals can live there. Cockroaches creep in damp and dark places—kitchen cabinets.

At night, when the humans have gone to sleep, cockroaches look for food scraps. As they search, they leave behind a stinking, oily liquid on kitchen counters. This may be a signal to other cockroaches. Or it may be to drive away predators like spiders. Small cockroach droppings are another sign of a cockroach's wanderings. They also leave behind a trail of bacteria.

It is little wonder that few people have a kind word to say for cockroaches. In Germany, one type of common cockroach is called the "Russian cockroach." In Russia, it is called the "German cockroach." Neither country wants to claim the common cockroach as its own. Actually, that cockroach probably came from Asia.

The Silver Starch-eater

An animal that can eat paper, linen, flour, and food scraps should thrive in a house. Add to this menu the glue in bookbindings and wallpaper paste, and a house is a supermarket for the silverfish.

Unlike the monster silverfish in the story, silverfish do not come out into the light. Maybe you've seen one of them running for cover after you've opened a cabinet.

Silverfish have shiny scales that give the insect a smooth and slippery texture. Slippery scales make it hard for predators to catch them.

Silverfish lay their eggs in small clusters in damp places. These may be cracks in cupboards, behind walls, or in musty old books. The next time you borrow an old book, watch out! You might bring home some new six-legged friends.

A Book in the Microwave?

Other book-eaters are booklice. These normally wingless insects eat the starch in bookbindings. They also eat the molds that grow on the yellowed pages of forgotten old paperbacks.

A way to rid books of booklice is to put the infested books into a microwave for 30 seconds. Even the lousiest book will be much improved!

Gross Feeders

The next time you see a housefly crawling on food, take a closer look. Extending from its head is a mouth-like organ called a proboscis. The fly uses its proboscis to mop the food with liquid from its gut. This liquid makes the food soupy and easy to digest. The fly then soaks up its liquid meal.

You can see where a fly has been

feeding by the light-colored specks on the food. Dark-colored specks are droppings the fly has left behind.

If you think that a fly on your food isn't so bad, remember this: the fly may have just been laying eggs on dog droppings or a pile of trash.

Each female can lay 150 eggs at a time. Within a day, the eggs hatch into wriggling maggots. After stuffing themselves on animal droppings or rotting food for a few days, each maggot becomes a pupa. About four days later, adult flies emerge. They mate within the hour. Flies may reach the ripe old age of one month.

House-eaters

A house is full of mouths—sucking, biting, and chewing. All are chowing down on whatever their owners call "food." To some, this food isn't found _in_ the house. Rather, it _is_ the house. To be precise, it is the house's wooden frame or floor.

Many homeowners carefully paint or wallpaper a wall. Then they sit back to admire

> pupa: An insect changing from a worm-like form to a flying form.

the finished job. They are unaware that a couple of inches away the wall is being destroyed.

Put a supersensitive microphone against a wall that has termites. It will pick up the sounds of hundreds of little feet running along. These feet, of course, belong to termites. Termites are insects with a taste for wood.

One type of termite tunnels into the house from their underground nest. They chew their way through wooden foundations. Then they start on the house's wooden frame.

If the house foundations are concrete, termites build little mud tubes up the sides of the concrete. Through these tubes, worker termites hurry back and forth. They are collecting and carrying gutfuls of wood to the nest.

As food goes, wood is not easy to digest. It's not all that nutritious either. In fact, termites only *eat* the wood. Tiny microbes in their guts digest it.

Termite Queen

microbes: Tiny, living things, such as bacteria.

Deep in a termite nest lies the queen termite. The queen's inch-long body produces egg after egg, every day for 20 years.

The queen is unable to move or feed herself. She is tended by dozens of worker termites. Workers spit up digested wood for her.

Standing alongside the queen are soldier termites. They have huge jaws and heads. Their job is to watch for enemies. The soldiers, too, are fed by the busy, wood-munching workers.

So completely do termites devour wood that after they're done, the wood crumbles into dust. By the time the homeowners know about the termites, it's too late to care about the color of the walls.

Look What the Cat Dragged In

To a flea, a cat or dog is a mobile home. A flea's thin, wingless body is ideal for walking in the forest of animal hair. As it walks, the flea searches for a spot to pierce the skin for a drink of blood.

The female cat flea lays about 500 eggs over a few months. The eggs fall off the cat and onto the place where the cat sleeps. Two days later, they hatch. Little white grubs come out to feed on dead skin or dried blood. Grubs hate light. So

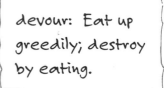

devour: Eat up greedily; destroy by eating.

they head for the carpet or for cracks in the wall. A couple of weeks later, each grub spins a cocoon. The cocoons may sit for months waiting.

When the family cat comes by, adult fleas appear from the cocoon to hitch a ride. If they can't find a cat, a human will do. The spread of killer human diseases, such as bubonic plague, owes much to the flea. But that's another story.

Imagine . . .

it is late winter in the year 1606 in the English town of Milford.

"Tom, Tom, you must come home—quickly, mother is dying!"

Jack Prescott was out of breath as he stood in the open doorway of the blacksmith's shop.

Tom, 13-year-old apprentice to his uncle, the blacksmith, looked up. Then he rushed to grab his brother.

"The Plague?"

Jack's sobbing confirmed Tom's fears.

The apprentice turned to his master who nodded permission for him to go. Tom tore off his leather apron, took Jack's hand, and stepped out into the cold.

Ever since Tom could remember, his town had been cursed by a dreadful disease. Hundreds of townsfolk had died in the past few months. Some people had fled the town. Most stayed indoors, going out into the chill only to search for food and firewood.

Tom and his brother walked quickly along the narrow cobbled lanes. They carefully dodged the piles of rotting vegetables and dead animals. Here and there were the contents of bedpans, thrown out windows above. The smell was sickening. They had to be careful not to slip on the filth.

Tom quickened his pace as a cart entered from a side lane. The cart was drawn by a bone-thin mule. The driver wore a cloak and a mask. Tom recognized the cart as the one that had carried away his father's dead body, and the corpses of a dozen neighbors.

Was a place waiting on that cart for his mother? For him? An icy shiver went through Tom at the thought.

Tom and Jack weren't the only ones to get out of the cart's way. Some large black rats that had been eating garbage, disappeared into a doorway.

The main street of Milford was empty, except for a beggar picking trash and the man with the cart. The sounds of Tom and Jack's footsteps and crows fighting over a dead dog echoed through the quiet town.

Tom still had nightmares about his father's cries of pain and the weeping black ulcer under his arm. The picture of his father's swollen body being tossed onto the cart still haunted Tom. Only two days before death, his father had been as strong as a bull.

No doctor would come to his father's aid, not without being paid like a king. Tom's family could only afford a medicine of herbs and mercury to draw out the sickness.

Even that had cost a month's wages. Now, his mother was dying.

Tom was now the man of the house. He felt a weight of responsibility.

Tom and Jack reached the open sewer that took the town's waste to the river. The boys held their sleeves to their faces to block the smell.

In summer, local boys would stand on the rickety wooden bridge that crossed the channel. They threw stones at the rats that used the sewer as a road into town. Tom and Jack lived just over the bridge.

The Prescott house was like all the others crowded on the edge of Milford. It was woodframed with mud walls. The boys entered the dark house. They climbed the stairs to their mother's room.

Tom went in and found his sister sobbing. Their mother was dead. Tom reached across to touch her.

It was then that he noticed the swelling under his arm. . . .

Chapter 2

Animals and Disease

Ring a round of rosies,
A pocket full of posies,
Ashes, ashes,
We all fall down.

THIS WELL-KNOWN nursery rhyme may seem like nonsense. But it has a very dark origin. The rhyme is about one of the most feared diseases in history—the bubonic plague, usually just called *the Plague*. This is the disease that killed Tom's mother and father in the story. It has taken millions of human lives over the centuries.

What Causes Bubonic Plague?

For over 1,500 years, people had no idea what caused the Plague. The man who collected the corpses wore a mask with flowers in the nosepiece. The pocket full of posies in the nursery rhyme did not protect him. But the smell of the flowers pushed back the smell of death.

It wasn't until 1894 that Alexander Yersin discovered the cause. It was a bacterium now called *Yersinia pestis*. For *Yersinia*, a human being is simply a place to live, feed, and reproduce. How this bacterium spread from victim to victim wasn't discovered until 1914.

How Does the Plague Spread?

The people of Milford and of other 17th century towns tried all kinds of folk medicines. These included putting mixtures on the skin to draw out illness. The rats of Milford were not suspected of being involved with the Plague. But, in fact, they had a lot to do with it.

Living conditions in 17th century Europe were not very sanitary. No one knew bacteria existed, let alone that bacteria cause disease. Waste (including human waste) was dumped in public streets. In such an environment, the black rat thrived.

Rats, Fleas, and People

The Plague bacterium lives in the blood of its host. Fleas feed on the blood of rats and other rodents. When a flea feeds on an infected rat, the bacteria are drawn into the gut of the flea that is drinking. The flea then infects the next animal on which it feeds. The filth of the times made ideal conditions for the fleas to breed. Eventually, people were bitten by infected fleas.

During the 14th century alone, the Plague killed 25 million people in Europe. That was one third of the entire population.

How Do People Die of the Plague?

Death by bubonic plague is horrifying. After a bite from an infected flea, bacteria enter the lymphatic system of the victim.

Within a few hours, the victim develops a fever and a headache. Then the bacteria cause the lymph glands under the arms and in the groin to swell into painful buboes.

Sometimes a dark pus-making sore appears at the site of the flea bite. The victim becomes confused and suffers chills and high fever. Within days, the patient dies of blood poisoning or lung infection.

lymphatic system: Body system that drains waste fluid.

buboes: Painful swellings of the lymph glands.

Where Did the Plague Come From?

The plague spread through Europe in the 1300s. It probably had its origins in Asia, around the borders of India, Burma, and China. *Yersinia pestis* had infected the local rats in this area.

Natural barriers, such as rivers, might have kept the bacterium from spreading. However, in the mid-1200s, Mongols invaded Europe from the East. Without knowing it, these invaders carried infected rats and fleas to the towns of eastern Europe. Then traders, without knowing, carried diseased rats westward on ships, carts, and carriages.

Plagues of the Future?

Today, unlike the 17th century, the connection between animals and disease is well known. People know that disease can be prevented by keeping their house and their body clean.

Throughout the world, there are diseases still isolated by natural barriers. If these barriers are broken down, those diseases will be free to spread. As humans move more and more into wild habitats, who knows what other diseases will be released?

Hong Kong Chicken Kill

In late 1997, the Hong Kong government ordered the death of about 1.6 million chickens. The reason? A virus carried by chickens had infected humans. Eighteen people became infected. Five died.

The disease had to be stopped. The job was so urgent the government ordered over 1,000 office workers to gas the chickens. When there was no more gas, chickens' necks were slit. People were asked to kill pet chickens. The government even offered to send someone to do it if killing a pet was too difficult for the owner. Other countries banned chicken imported from Hong Kong.

Experts were flown in to investigate the situation. Tests were carried out on cats and dogs that had eaten chicken. Fear of the disease led some people to kill any bird, not just chickens. In the end, the virus was controlled.

Mad Cow Madness

CJD (Creutzfeldt-Jacob disease) is a fatal disease that attacks the human brain. Sufferers quickly develop spasms, lose coordination, and become confused. CJD is rare. About 10 people per year got the disease in the early 1970s. By the 1990s, this number had increased to about 35.

BSE (bovine spongiform encephalopathy) is a disease similar to CJD. BSE attacks the brain of cattle. It causes their brain cells to become sponge-like. Animals with BSE wander around as if they are drunk. This is why BSE is called "mad cow disease."

The Connection Is . . .

Scientists believe that cows got mad cow disease from eating dried cattle meal. The cattle meal was made from the guts and brains of sheep. Some of the sheep had scrapie. Scrapie is a disease that attacks the brain of sheep. It makes them constantly scrape or rub against the nearest solid object.

It wasn't long before a question was asked. If cows can catch a brain disease from eating dead sheep, can humans catch a brain disease from eating dead cows? A scientific report published in 1996 said that 60 people had died of CJD. The report said that the people had gotten the disease by eating beef from cows with mad cow disease. The deaths had all occurred in Britain. Panic swept the UK.

British Beef Banned

The British beef industry was in trouble. Foreign countries banned British beef. McDonald's in Britain imported Dutch beef. Even British Airways took British beef off the in-flight menu.

The British government denied that there was a link between CJD and mad cow disease. Now Britain was under pressure to slaughter thousands of its cattle before the bans would be lifted.

The Solution?

Between 1970 and 1998, as many as 755 people may have died from eating the meat of mad cows. Public concern was great. Mass cattle slaughters tried to get rid of the problem. Worldwide bans on British beef were imposed.

Still, at the end of March 1996, many stores in Britain reported that people bought ten times as much beef, when the price was cut 50 percent. As one shopper said, "I know it's a risk, but it's worth it at this price."

It was never proved that CJD was passed on by eating beef.

Rabies

The expression "foaming at the mouth" is used to describe someone mad with rage. The saying comes from that dreaded disease, rabies. Rabies is caused by a virus that infects mammals and humans. What does rabies do?

In March 1998, a man in northern Russia was attacked by a wolf. Healthy wolves do not normally attack humans. So, bites to his head, hands, and legs were thoroughly cleaned. Injections of rabies vaccine were given for three days.

However, 25 days later, the man became very ill. Spasms in his throat were so painful that he couldn't drink. In fact, he became terrified of water. He was mentally confused. And he developed a high fever. He died six days later of heart failure and brain seizure.

Method in the Madness

The rabies virus infects its host's brain. Like all viruses, the rabies virus must spread from one host to another to survive. So how does it get from the brain of one host to the brain of another?

First, the virus spreads to the saliva of its host. When the host bites, the saliva infects a new victim. The more animals the host bites, the more infection spreads. A major effect of the virus is to make its host aggressive. A rabid dog is a "mad dog" that foams at the mouth and attacks. A dripping mouth, in a dog that bites, makes perfect conditions for rabies to spread.

Rabies is still a problem in most countries. In North America, the disease is most common in skunks, foxes, bats, raccoons, dogs, and cats. One country, Australia, has managed to keep the rabies virus out. Being an island has helped Australia keep control. All animals are tested for rabies before they are allowed into the country.

saliva: A liquid-like substance in the mouth; spit.

What About Parasites?

To parasites, the human body is just another warm place to breed and eat. A parasite is a tiny plant or animal that feeds off another plant or animal without doing anything to help its host. Humans detest and fear parasites with good reason. Parasites can cause horrible diseases.

It's a Fluke!

About 200 million people in Africa, Asia, and South America are infested by a parasite. The troublemaker is a type of flatworm—the blood fluke. The blood fluke damages the liver, bladder, lungs, and intestines of its victims. Victims become so weak they easily catch a serious disease and die.

The Amazing Journey of the Blood Fluke

Adult blood flukes live in the blood vessels near the intestines of infested humans. About an inch long, flukes use suckers to stick to the walls of the blood vessels. There they take in nutrients from the blood.

When they are ready to produce eggs, flukes push their way inside the capillaries of the intestinal

capillaries: Small blood vessels.

36

wall. The flukes lay so many eggs that the capillaries burst. The eggs move into the intestine. There they are bound for the outside world along with the human waste. If the waste is dropped where the eggs can reach the water supply, the eggs live on.

Snails?

When they reach the water supply, the fluke eggs hatch. The swimming larvae seek out a particular type of snail. The larvae dig into the flesh of a snail and feed on it. The larvae then reproduce.

The new flukes leave the snail and swim around in search of their next host. That could be somebody walking in a lake. Once on the skin, the flukes eat their way through to a blood vessel. Eventually, they find their way to the blood vessels of the intestine. This completes their journey.

Many diseases that once killed people are now under control. But the human body is warm, moist, and made of flesh and blood. So it will always attract disease-causing creatures.

larvae: Young worm-like form of a fluke; plural of larva.

Chapter 3: Introduction

Imagine . . .

you're diving in shark-infested waters.

"WHAT DID MOM SAY, Dad?"

"I'm not sure, Andy. I can't hear her over the seals."

The boat bobbed on the water 20 yards from the rocks, where hundreds of seals argued over positions.

"I don't think I'd like to be a seal, Dad. It looks too uncomfortable."

"Yeah, and cold, too. Your mom and Jim won't be able to stay too long out there—even with wetsuits."

"This has been a great trip, Dad. We've seen whales, dolphins, and now seals. Do you think any of them will go into the water?"

Until that moment, Andy's father hadn't really noticed that no seals were swimming. They were all on the rocks. He turned to his son. Then, he looked back at the sea. He cupped his hands to his mouth, and called.

"Linda! . . . Linda! . . . Jim!"

"What is it, Dad? What's the matter?" Andy was puzzled by his father's panic.

"Give me the binoculars—quick!"

Andy found the binoculars and held them up for his father. He didn't understand why his dad was so uptight all of a sudden. He surely couldn't have been worried about Mom. She was a very experienced diver. And she was with Jim Brown, the best diving coach in the country, according to Mom.

Dad must be a little overprotective, that's all, thought Andy.

"There's Mom, by those rocks."

"Where, where?" Andy's father swung the binoculars wildly from side to side.

Andy steadied his father's hands and

steered them in his mother's direction.

"There. Do you see her now?"

He did see her, about forty yards away. Linda's mask was pulled up to her forehead and her arm was waving. She blew them both a kiss. Jim must have still been underwater.

Andy watched his father's fear give way to smiling relief. He turned to Andy.

"Sorry, Andy, I just got a little—"

All relief disappeared as a horrible scream cut the sea air. For a moment, all other sounds were muted. The barking of the seals, the slapping of the sea, the cries of the gulls, and the waves breaking on the rocks were silent. The scream was the only sound.

"Oh, no, oh, no. Andy, quick, start the motor."

Andy fumbled with the starter cord. His father trained the binoculars on the spot he had last seen his wife.

"I can't see her! I can't see her!"

Andy felt guilty. Why hadn't he taken his father's concern seriously?

Andy's father steered the boat toward the rocks. He cut the motor.

"Linda!"

Suddenly, Andy's mother surfaced by the boat.

She was sobbing as Andy helped his father haul her from the water. She leaned over the side of the boat. Her eyes darted over the sea around her.

"Where's Jim? We have to find him!"

All three were now watching the sea.

The water in front of the boat was moving differently. The steady chop of the waves was gone. The surface was swirling and smooth.

Then, a great boiling up of water began. Its color changed as it bubbled. Pink. Then darker. And then. . . .

Andy and his parents watched in horror as the boiling erupted in red blood. Then a human face emerged from the sea. The face had no expression—no recognition of the three watching. The face had no life.

Andy would always remember that final scene. It seemed as if it had lasted an hour. But, he knew that it had been only a moment.

Only a moment until the great gray shape finally claimed its prey. . . .

Chapter 3

Animals That Attack

IN THE SEA, a human is a slow-moving animal. A shark is fast and strong with rows of razor-sharp teeth. Imagine what a shark attack would be like and you can get a sense of pure fear. It's utter helplessness in the face of overwhelming power.

The waters near seal colonies are hunting grounds for great white sharks. They target seals that are slow or young. A healthy alert seal is too quick a swimmer for a great white. A human swimmer in a wetsuit probably looks to a shark like a very slow sick seal.

The great white shark can grow to 20 feet in length. The tallest human is not even half that length.

What we call a shark attack is to the shark simply a matter of finding something to eat. Hopefully, it is something that won't take too much work to catch. Animals "attack" people when they are hungry or when they feel threatened.

Conflict Between Humans and Animals

The chance of an animal attacking a human becomes greater as more humans come into contact with animals. When an animal attacks a person, people forget that the person has probably entered the animal's territory. Yet the animal is often seen as the one at fault.

A century ago, there were large wilderness areas. The animals that lived there rarely met people. Today, much of this wilderness has disappeared. More and more people are visiting the wild areas that remain. Conflict between animals and humans is bound to happen. Being near animals increases the likelihood of being attacked. Provoking them can guarantee it.

Provoking an animal can be as simple as trying to get close to take a photo. For example, most bison attacks occur when the animal feels threatened. A tourist who doesn't understand that the bison is a wild animal can end up in great danger.

Do People Ask to Be Attacked?

provoke: To cause anger or action.

Taking a photo may be a mild way to provoke an animal. Forcing your will on an animal is more serious.

Often humans deliberately try to control animals.

A circus is a place where many wild animals are forced to behave unnaturally. This puts the animals under stress, and they may react violently.

Circus Elephant Panic

During a performance of the Circus International in Honolulu in 1994, people in the audience saw a horrifying event. An African elephant called Tyke suddenly crushed her trainer, killing him. Tyke severely injured another circus worker and a dozen spectators. Then she charged out of the arena and headed downtown.

The animal was no doubt confused and very frightened. She ran through the streets for half an hour. Police fired more than a 100 shots at Tyke before she collapsed. It took three more shots to kill her. Animals such as Tyke are often called "rogue animals," as if they're to blame.

In England, at Howlett's Wild Animal Park, it was usual

for keepers to enter the tiger cage. At that zoo, a Siberian tiger killed its keeper with a single bite. After the deadly attack, the zoo's owner said that the animal had inherited a "mean streak" from its mother. (She herself had killed two keepers.) The owner didn't say that the tiger had not been fed for four days. A desperate, starving tiger could see a zookeeper as a meal.

The Risk of Living with Wild Animals?

In one part of India, an average of 40 people a year are killed by tigers. The region is home to 100,000 people. They make their living by fishing, collecting firewood, and harvesting honey. One resident was asked about the danger. He replied, "You townspeople are run over by buses. We are sometimes killed by wild beasts."

Casualties of War

An animal attack on a large scale occurred during World War II. British troops had trapped almost 1,000 Japanese soldiers on an island off the coast of Burma. During the night, the Japanese troops tried to cross a swamp to reach the sea and escape.

Of the 1,000 Japanese, only about 20 survived. It wasn't shooting that killed them, though. What no one knew was that the swamp was filled with saltwater crocodiles, the largest crocodiles of all. In the dark, and with no place to run, the soldiers were easy prey.

Man-eating Lions?

Lions usually stay away from humans. But sometimes food is scarce. Sometimes a lion is hurt or too old to catch its usual food. Then humans may become targets.

In 1898, a pair of male lions preyed on workers who were building a bridge in Kenya. Before the lions were shot, they had killed at least 130 men. This event was made into a movie called *The Ghost and the Darkness*.

What Exactly Is an Animal Attack?

When we say an animal has attacked someone, what do we mean? There probably wouldn't be any argument that the crocodiles, shark, elephant, and tiger mentioned earlier all attacked people. These animals deliberately injured or killed their human victims.

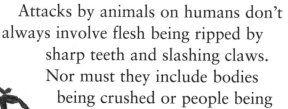

Attacks by animals on humans don't always involve flesh being ripped by sharp teeth and slashing claws. Nor must they include bodies being crushed or people being gored by horns or antlers. Insects, spiders, and other small animals account for most of the attacks by animals on humans.

Attacked by Maggots

A trip to a Brazilian rain forest might mean a traveler should watch out for jaguars or even anacondas. Flies might not be considered a threat. However, in 1998, a man from Alabama returned from a trip to Brazil with sores on his head. The

gored: Stabbed by something pointed.

sores grew daily. A doctor examined the sores and found screwworm maggots feeding on the man's scalp. A screwworm fly must have laid her eggs in a cut on the man's head. Had the maggots not been found, they would have kept eating the man's scalp tissue. Until they became adult flies.

Stingers

From November to April, the tropical waters off the north coast of Australia are off-limits to swimmers. The reason—box jellyfish. The adult jellyfish has a 5-inch top end (the "bell") and 10-foot tentacles. The box jellyfish (or sea wasp or fire medusa) is one of the most dangerous creatures in the sea.

The tentacles trail behind as the box jellyfish swims. Thousands of stingers inject a deadly venom into the small fish and shellfish the jellyfish feeds on. If the tentacles brush a human body, the venom is injected in the same way. It feels like a burn by a blow torch. The results are often fatal. Would you call this an animal "attack?"

A Pet Wouldn't Attack. . . . Would It?

Maybe you will never hear of a pet goldfish attacking someone. But attacks by pets on humans are common.

Many people share their homes with carnivores—meat eaters. Look at your dog's teeth. The four large, pointed canine teeth are for killing and tearing prey. At one time, all dogs were wild. Their survival depended on using these teeth to kill and eat prey. Pet dogs still have these teeth. And they can still behave like their wild ancestors.

Do Fighting Dogs Make Good Pets?

Humans have used the hunting skills of dogs to their own benefit. Guard dogs are used to protect property. Police dogs help catch criminals. These animals are trained to attack people. Some people even keep such animals as pets.

Some dog breeds are more likely than others to attack people. People have bred them that way. For example, guard dogs are bred from animals that are naturally more aggressive than other dogs. Likewise, tracking dogs have been bred from animals that have a very sharp sense of smell.

Pit Bull: Dangerous or Misunderstood?

The American pit bull terrier was bred from English breeds that were fighting dogs. Several centuries ago these dogs were bred to fight bears or bulls for public entertainment.

Of course, pit bull terriers aren't *always* aggressive. They are just more likely than other dogs to be aggressive. Because of this, they have a fearsome reputation.

One pit bull attack involved a worker at an animal shelter in Maryland. The dog was in the shelter because it had attacked a child. The dog attacked the worker while he was cleaning out the dog's cage. The attack was so violent that his hand was almost completely severed. It took three operations to attach the hand again.

Why Do Animals Attack?

To explain why any animal attacks a person requires an understanding of the animal's nature.

Humans see the world in terms of themselves. For example, if a crocodile kills a tourist, we think that the crocodile is a monster. It should be destroyed. From the crocodile's point of view, it was simply hunting for a meal. Or maybe it was defending its territory.

In Australia in 1997, a dog, Fizo, was given an award for bravery after it killed a snake. It had "saved the lives of four children." Think of this situation from the snake's point of view. With four children and a dog coming toward it, the snake most likely feared for its life.

Imagine . . .

you're in a dimly-lit shed getting ready to watch two animals fight to the death.

"**Y**OU CAN'T TELL ME that this ain't natural. There's nothin' more natural than two animals fightin'. 'Specially males fightin' over their territory or their females. So what's wrong with just having a little bet on the result, eh? They're gonna do it anyways."

"That's a pretty good looking bird you have there, Joe."

"Yeah, I call him 'The Tractor' 'cause he just keeps right on goin'."

I watched Joe as he stroked The Tractor. He seemed as loving as a child petting a teddy bear or a kitten. The Tractor jerked his head from side to side, the way roosters do. It clucked as Joe kissed its beak.

"Why don't you check to see if the crowd's buildin'."

I nodded. Then I pulled back the curtain that separated us from the low-fenced pit. This is where the action was about to take place.

We were in a shed behind a garage workshop. Benches made of boards resting on tin drums had been arranged for the crowd.

A dozen or so men had already arrived. They laughed and chatted as they waited. Some of them held birds under their arms.

I turned back to Joe, who was taping a one-inch spur to The Tractor's right leg. He had already fixed one to the bird's left leg.

Joe explained as he taped. "This here's the scorpion. It's finer than the piranha . . . cuts deeper."

Joe finished preparing his champion and placed it in its cage.

"Is he your favorite, Joe?" Joe looked at me in a way that said I'd asked the wrong question.

"You know, I usually don't have time for favorites. If I can get two, maybe three fights outta each bird, I'm happy. This'll be The Tractor's second match, so he's better than most.

"I reckon that if I keep him pumped up, he might go on a little longer. But if he don't, then he don't."

It was time for the first fight. We pulled back the curtain and entered the pit. By now there were about thirty men waiting. Most of them were seated. Some leaned against a workbench on the far side. Two very big men stood by the shed door.

Joe took The Tractor and held him at one corner of the pit. The Tractor was up against a similar-looking bird, with similar-looking spurs.

Then the birds noticed each other. Each struggled to get at the other. Ten or more roosters strutted in cages. Their owners and spectators laid bets. A lot of money was changing hands.

A loud and sweaty man, who, I think, was the referee, gave the order to let the birds go.

Joe held his rooster up to its opponent. The opponent was similarly held by its owner. The birds were desperate to attack.

When they were released, the birds launched at each other in a frenzy. The spurs flashed in a blurred confusion of feathers and beaks. I couldn't see the spurs strike. But strike they must have.

Within seconds, blood spurted from The Tractor. Then the other bird was bleeding. Surely the birds would stop. But these were fighting birds. They, too, were slaves to a powerful instinct that pays no attention to pain or the threat of death.

The spectators cheered. I couldn't understand why. They, too, seemed to be slaves to another instinct.

The Tractor was dead. His blood-soaked body lay in the dust as his opponent struggled just to stand.

I looked at Joe. I supposed he'd be upset. Instead he just shrugged.

"It was his day, son." . . .

Animals in Entertainment

HUMANS HAVE COMPLEX relationships with animals. We eat them. We pet them. We kill them. And we love them.

There is much argument about how animals should or should not be treated. The use of animals for entertainment is often hotly debated.

People Want to See Blood

Cockfighting is just one of many sports where animals fight. The gruesome attraction of these sports lies in seeing animals hurt each other. It also lies in the chance to gamble on the outcome.

Cockfighting began in India and Persia (Iran). As long ago as 500 B.C., there were cockfights in Greece. The birds used in cockfighting are not farmyard roosters, but gamecocks.

Gamecocks are specially-bred birds with long legs to thrust attached spurs into their opponents. Often the gamecocks' throats and breasts are shaved to make it easier for spurs to catch hold.

Owners may use artificial methods to prolong the "fight" in a bird. Injections of strychnine act as a stimulant. It causes birds to fight on even when they are seriously injured. Vitamin K may also be injected to reduce the amount of bleeding.

Cockfighting was banned in Britain in 1849 and is illegal in most U.S. states. Cockfighting is still legal in the Philippines and some other countries.

This Is More Than Just Badgering

Using animals for violent entertainment has been around for centuries. Badger baiting amused

spectators in the backyards of English taverns during the Middle Ages. It was outlawed in 1835.

In badger baiting, a wild badger is placed in a wooden box. Dogs are then placed in front of the box. The dogs are encouraged to attack the badger and pull it out of the box.

Bets are placed on whether a dog will succeed. The badger is usually chained. Sometimes, to increase a dog's chances, the badger's jaw is broken. Badger baiting contests still occur—illegally—in out-of-the-way locations.

Other blood sports include bull baiting and dogfighting. In bull baiting, now a thing of the past, a tied-up bull was attacked by dogs that were specially bred for the task. We know these breeds of dogs as bulldogs and bullterriers. In dogfighting, pit bull terriers or bullterriers are set against each other.

Fish Don't Fight. . . . Do They?

As long as there are animals that will fight, there will be people who watch and bet on the result. In

Thailand, this applies to fish as well as to roosters.

The 2-inch male Siamese fighting fish is brightly colored. When faced by a rival male, his color becomes even more vivid. In the wild, this color change warns off rivals before they need to fight. However, when a pair of fighting fish are forced together in a jar, there is no escape. They will attack each other. Fins and tails can be ripped apart as onlookers place bets on the result.

Ancient Roman Wild Beast Shows

A cockfight can seem a pretty tame affair when it's compared to the animal slayings in ancient Rome. In arenas such as the 50,000 seat Colosseum, thousands of animals met their deaths. There is a story of how a bear and a bull, chained together, fought to exhaustion.

Sometimes hundreds of animals, including leopards, lions, elephants, giraffes, bulls, and tigers, were released into the arena. The crowd would watch the animals attack each other.

Slaves, criminals, and Christians and other hated groups, would often be included in the bloody show.

Over 100,000 animals were captured in North Africa and the Middle East. Then they were shipped to Rome for this public entertainment. No doubt the animals were terrified to be put in front of so many cheering people. Other cities of the Roman Empire had their own arenas for wild beast shows.

Are There Still Wild Beast Shows?

Perhaps the closest thing today to Roman wild beast shows is the bullfight. This sport is over 4,000 years old. In Spain, bullfighting is part of the country's culture and tradition. However, many countries oppose bullfighting on the grounds that it is cruel.

A Modern Bullfight

A bullfight begins with the release of a healthy and fierce bull into the arena. As the crowd cheers, *banderilleros* enter the arena. The job of these men is to tease the bull, and make it charge. The

banderilleros
(ban-der-ree-air-os)

picador (pee-ka-door)

bull becomes frustrated as the banderilleros keep it running around the arena. The bull begins to tire.

Enter the *picador*, a bullfighter carrying a sharp-pointed spear. He rides on a heavily padded, blindfolded horse. The bull charges at the horse, sometimes knocking it down. When this happens, the banderilleros race out to distract the bull. The horse gets back on its feet.

As the bull tries to gore the horse, the picador stabs the spear between the bull's shoulders. He leans on the spear to drive it deeper. The wound weakens the bull's neck muscles. Now the bull charges with its head held low.

The banderilleros again take to the arena. This time they plunge darts into the wound made by the spear. The darts are attached to poles about three feet long. The darts stick in the wound, and the poles hang down, tearing the wound open. This further weakens the bull's neck. The bull is kept busy twisting and turning by the banderilleros during all this.

Enter the Star of the Show

By this time, the bull is bleeding from its gaping wound. It is close to exhaustion. Only now does the bull face the *matador.*

The matador is the star of the bullfight. He enters the ring and begins teasing the bull with his cape. The crowd roars its approval as the bull passes dangerously close to the matador's body again and again. As the bleeding bull tires, his charges become weaker.

The matador shows the sword to the crowd. The crowd cheers. The matador sidesteps the bull's last lunge. He drives his sword through the opening made by the spear and darts. It goes deep into the animal's chest. The bull staggers and falls.

The matador receives the crowd's applause. Men with daggers stab the bull to make sure it's dead. The dead bull is dragged away. The next bull is made ready to face its last 20 minutes.

Is Laughing at Animals Okay?

For most people, the sight of an animal being killed slowly is not good entertainment. Many people prefer to watch animals performing tricks. Elephants stand on their heads. Bears ride motorcycles. Lions jump through flaming hoops. These are just a few of the many tricks that humans train animals to perform.

In animal blood sports, humans exploit a natural behavior (to fight). With animal tricks, humans make animals do things for our amusement. For some people, a bear riding a motorbike is funny. They laugh when they see a chimpanzee dressed in clothes and trained to smoke. Not everyone finds these tricks amusing.

Animal Performers?

These tricks have nothing to do with the way an animal naturally behaves. Many people do not know that training animals to do tricks puts the animal under great stress.

A tiger's fear of fire is instinctive. Training a tiger to jump through a flaming hoop is unnatural. It also puts the tiger in a terrifying situation. When a tiger is frightened, it may hurt itself—or it may hurt its trainer. In this way, training animals to do tricks that are against their nature can be dangerous.

How Else Can Animals Entertain Us?

Wild beast shows, animal fighting, and circus tricks are forms of entertainment. They depend on interfering with an animal's nature. But people can also be entertained by an animal behaving naturally. For instance, a bird show in a zoo might feature a falcon swooping from a great height to catch a mouse from its keeper's hand. The audience would be amazed at the great speed of the bird as it dives.

Animals behaving naturally in their own environment can be amazing and powerful entertainment.

Chapter 5: Introduction

Imagine . . .

you are lost in a forest with nothing to eat.

W HAT A HORRIBLE VACATION! First, Dad forgets to lock the back door. We had to go all the way back home to lock it. Then he gets a speeding ticket when he tries to make up lost time.

Worst of all was my little sister Penelope. She dripped her disgusting chocolate milk all over my new jeans. But all this looks really unimportant now that we're lost.

We had stopped for a while so Dad could take a break from driving and have a nap. That's when Penelope decided to go for a walk in the woods. I went after her. When I found her, I had no idea how to get back. That was yesterday.

It's really awful being stuck in the middle of

nowhere with someone you can't stand. Penelope got us lost in the first place. But now I had to look after her.

"I'm hungry."

"Well, so am I, Penelope. Stop your whining."

Little sisters are the worst. I know I wasn't like her when I was a two-year-old.

Actually, though, we *were* very hungry. We'd already spent one night in this endless forest without food. We hadn't eaten for 24—no—27 hours! I could really go for a burger, or even one of Dad's stupid stews! Well, maybe not that.

"Come on, Penelope, let's go."

Of course, I had no idea where we were going. Maybe there were some berries around or something. There certainly wasn't anything where we were.

"They'll find us soon, Penelope. Then we can eat and eat and eat all we want."

Penelope didn't answer. I turned and she wasn't there.

"Penelope, where are you?"

Great. We were lost and hungry, and now Penelope had decided to wander off again.

There was a rustle in the undergrowth and Penelope appeared. I was angry. She was smiling and chewing!

"What are you eating?"

She held out her hand and opened her fingers. There, curled up in her chubby little palm, were three small, disgusting white grubs. They had little legs that waved in the air and fat glistening bodies.

"Oh, Penelope, that's gross."

I slapped her hand and sent the grubs flying. Penelope stared at me. Then her face crinkled. She began to cry and then started screaming. The last time she screamed like that was when the strawberry ice cream fell off her cone at the kindergarten party.

"All right, all right. Here, I'll pick them up for you."

I hunted around on my hands and knees in the grass, searching for those hideous creatures. Beside me another hideous creature stood and sobbed.

As I gave her each grub, Penelope immediately shoved it into her mouth. She would munch it furiously. It was as if I was passing her candy. She couldn't get enough of them. All I could do every time she ate one of those disgusting things was groan. How could she?

She must have eaten a dozen.

The smile returned to Penelope's little face. I forced a smile back at her.

"Why are you eating those grubs?"

"They're yummy. Let's get some more."

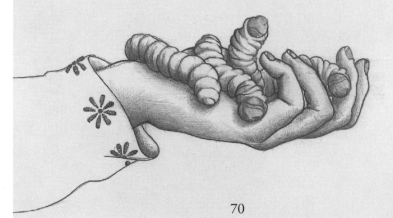

Penelope took me by the hand. I let her lead me back through the brush. We stopped at a rotten log. Penelope knelt next to it. She dug her fingers into the rotting wood and pulled off a loose piece.

There, lying at the ends of wooden tunnels they had eaten for themselves, lay ten or more of Penelope's disgusting grubs. She got to work digging them out. She collected three or four and, can you believe it, she offered them to me!

"Here, for you." . . .

Chapter 5

Animals We Eat

Would you eat a grub, or an insect, or a snail? Little children don't know any better. Toddlers even eat dirt! Of course, by the time they get older, they do know better. Or do they?

What Foods Do You Eat?

What we eat depends on where we were born. For example, if you grew up in Italy, you might eat a lot of pasta. If you grew up in India, you might eat rice, and in Japan, fish. We learn to like the foods of the country we live in.

What Animals Do You Eat?

Why are cattle (beef), sheep (mutton and lamb), pigs (bacon, ham, and pork), chickens, and fish so popular? Are they tastier than other animals?

Maybe they're popular because we know how to raise a lot of them. And they are cheap to buy. Yet there are a lot of insects, spiders, and worms around, but we don't eat them.

Does Anyone Eat Insects?

Eating insects isn't a new fad. It's been going on in many countries for centuries.

Aboriginal people of southeastern Australia liked to eat the bogong moth. This insect swarms to the mountains in early summer. There, thousands of them rest in rocky crevices and caves. The southeast Aborigines would follow the moths to the mountains and spend the summer feasting on them.

Did the moths make a healthful feast? Each moth is up to 60 percent fat, with some carbohydrate and protein. But, it has been reported that this rich food caused some digestive problems for the Aborigines.

To cook the moths, the native people tossed the insects on hot ashes. The moths were cooked just long enough to slightly burn the wings and legs. Moths that weren't eaten right away were cooked and squashed together in fatty lumps for eating later. And the taste? Sweet and nutty.

aboriginal: Native.

Aborigines: Native people of Australia.

Aborigines of the central deserts find moth larvae particularly tasty. The fat, white grub is about three inches long. It is considered a special treat that can be eaten raw. When lightly cooked, it tastes like roast pork.

Another tasty insect, found in central Australia, is the honeypot ant. Some honeypot ants act as living honey jars. They store nectar for their fellow workers. Their abdomen swells like a tiny balloon. People bite off the abdomen to enjoy the sweet contents.

Are Insects Good for You?

Dried insects can be up to 75 percent protein. That's not bad when compared to dried beef, which is only 40 percent protein. And most insects have very little fat.

A popular Mexican dish is made from escamoles, the grubs of a certain black ant. (Some people use the eggs instead.) The grubs are fried with onions and garlic and eaten in tacos.

A French favorite is chocolate-covered ants.

abdomen: The main body part of an insect; the trunk.

74

Have You Eaten Insects?

You might know the story of the old woman who swallowed a fly. The idea of an insect that likes garbage crawling around inside us is not a nice one.

What about the insects we don't know we ate? You would probably notice a shiny brown cockroach walking on a green lettuce leaf. No doubt you would remove it. But what about little green things? Would you notice them?

Much of the food we eat has insect parts in it. Brown flecks in bread may be parts of flour beetles caught up in the dough! But don't worry! A few insect parts won't hurt you. They might actually be good for you.

How About Eight-Legged Creatures?

Order a spider in Cambodia and you will probably get a tasty little pastry with a four-inch spider buried inside.

What about lobster and shrimp? They're not insects or spiders. But they're not far from it. They have many legs and a hard external skeleton. If animals like that are a special treat, why wouldn't a grasshopper be the same?

Can Food be Dangerous?

In Japan, most food poisoning is the result of eating a popular dish—fugu puffer fish. This is a toxic fish that only skilled chefs can prepare properly. It takes a 30-step process to leave just enough of the fish's toxin. Just a hint of toxin and diners enjoy a mild tingling of the lips and a slight light-headedness. Too much toxin means death.

Which Parts Do You Eat?

Let's get back to sheep, cattle, pigs, chickens, and fish. Many people think these animals are okay to eat, but not just any part of them. Meat, which is muscle, is the preferred part. You can easily find steak on a menu. But what about tongue, or brain, or nose? Are these so weird? They come from the same animals, after all.

Many people find the idea of eating anything except the meat sickening. Yet, organ meats—liver, heart, and kidneys—still sell in supermarkets.

Maybe it's because organ meats are red, so they look like meat. Tripe, which is cow or sheep stomach, is not nearly as popular. Tripe is creamy white.

Maybe what turns people off is knowing the body part. You might try a traditional haggis if you visited Scotland. Would you eat it if you knew it was "a sheep's stomach stuffed with heart, liver, and lungs?"

There's a lot to be said for eating more than just the muscle tissue of an animal. Think of how much of a cow is wasted if we eat only the muscle. And the muscle is not always the most healthful part of an animal. Organ meats usually have less fat and more nutrients than a hamburger or steak. So, next time you have a craving for meat, why not try a nice sheep's brain . . . or a slice of cow's liver? Who knows—you might just like it!

Where's the Beef?

Many people believe that our meat-eating habit is not friendly to the environment. For instance, it takes ten acres of farm land to feed two people beef. The same ten acres can feed 24 people wheat.

Unfortunately, not all land is suitable for growing wheat or other grains. And grains alone do not provide the protein necessary for a well-balanced diet. On the other hand, most grasslands are suitable for grazing cattle. That might explain why cattle are raised in almost every country. In total, there are 1.4 billion cattle in the world.

Why Not Eat Dogs and Cats?

No relationship between humans and animals is more confusing than how we choose which animals we eat and which animals we make pets. In Korea, some people eat dog meat. Many people in Western countries find this alarming. They can't imagine killing and eating "man's best friend."

Many people here accept the fact that ham comes from pigs, and find it okay that beef comes from cows. Yet, many others believe that cows are sacred and pigs are unclean.

Should We Eat Any Animals We Choose?

Different cultures have different favorite animals for food. Does this mean that all animals are fair game for the kitchen? What about whales?

Japan and Norway still hunt whales. The minke whale is hunted in great numbers now that other whale species are endangered. To many people in Iceland, Greenland, and the Faroe Islands, whale meat is a traditional dish.

What about gorillas and chimpanzees? In central Africa, where these primates are found, there is a thriving trade

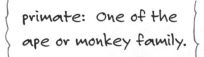
primate: One of the ape or monkey family.

in "bushmeat." Apes and monkeys are hunted for their meat. The meat is not cheap. The money to be made encourages hunters to continue.

People in Africa have eaten these animals for centuries. But only recently has it become available in restaurants. Whether it is acceptable to eat these animals is not the important issue. What is important is whether these animals will survive if they continue to be hunted.

A Changing Menu

What we choose to eat is influenced by our cultural background. Our taste in meat, whether it be insect, mammal, or bird, is a matter of personal choice.

The world is becoming smaller. People are moving from country to country. And they are taking their eating habits with them. We are now able to try a greater variety of food than ever before. What you find delicious, your grandparents may never have seen. Maybe one day, grasshoppers or grubs will be on your list of favorite foods—if they aren't already!

Chapter 6: Introduction

Imagine . . .

it's the first day of summer vacation at your uncle's farm in Australia.

It's a dusty road that leads from town to Uncle Bob's farm. And it's a rough ride, especially in the back of an old truck.

This was the third summer that I had traveled over 24 hours to get to my uncle's farm in Australia. I was looking forward to a summer of sheep herding, fence building, and fun. But there was nothing like that ride to remind me that I was back.

Like the last two summers, my mouth was full of road grit before we got far from the station. The country was yellow and dry. Clusters of sheep were standing here and there in the bare fields. I couldn't understand how anyone or anything could survive in such a dry place.

By the look of it, only the rabbits were doing well. They were everywhere.

The truck bounced on. I felt myself slipping into my summer world. It was a world away from the noise and crowd of school and the city back home. I watched the dust billow behind the truck in boiling red clouds. Then something caught my eye. I looked to the right, to the fence that ran along the road. I wasn't ready for what I saw.

Dad says that the greatest tragedies are those where the once-proud are beaten down. The 30 eagles stretched, wing tip to wing tip, along that fence were like that— once proud. (Later Uncle Bob told me that it was 28.)

I stood to look at the sorry sight as the truck slowed for rough road. What could have happened? Were these birds victims of some horrible accident? Surely they wouldn't have been shot. Would they? I felt as if a cold wind had just blown in on my vacation. I sat back down as the truck got going again.

Lunch was ready when we arrived at Uncle Bob's. Aunt Dotty had, as always, prepared a feast of roast lamb, peas, potatoes, and carrots. This was usually the first highlight of the summer. But this year, my appetite had deserted me. Uncle Bob noticed my uneasy mood.

"Hey, you're a quiet one this year, Tim. Missing your mother already?" Uncle Bob chuckled. He liked teasing.

I shot him a weak smile.

"Of course he's not, Robert. He's thirteen. More peas, Timmy?"

"Uh, no thanks, Aunt Dotty."

I turned to Uncle Bob and decided to say what was bothering me.

"Uncle Bob, those eagles back on the—"

"So that's what's bothering you, Tim."

Uncle Bob seemed a little angry.

"Look, Tim, this has been a hard year. A lot of lambs have been taken."

Uncle Bob was waving his fork at me and was talking with his mouth full. Aunt Dotty frowned at him. So did I.

"Well, what am I supposed to do—let the place be taken over by birds?

"You see, Tim, the balance has been upset. The country is full of sheep now. That's the way it is. And the eagles have done all right from it. Now there are too many eagles. We need to get the balance right. Gee, I'm not going to kill all of them, now am I?"

Aunt Dotty said nothing. She just cleared the table. I sat quietly as Uncle Bob continued.

"Now, we've just got to get those darn rabbits under control." . . .

Chapter 6

Animals and Folklore

During the 1950s, the government in Queensland, Australia, offered hunters a reward for shooting Australia's largest bird of prey, the wedge-tailed eagle. The reason? The eagles were hunting sheep. In one year, 12,000 rewards were paid. Dead eagle bodies were proudly hung on barbed-wire fences. It was a sign that the problem was being addressed.

However, studies later showed that the eagles weren't actually killing the sheep. More than 80 percent of an eagle's diet was the European rabbit, the number one pest of Australian farming.

By shooting eagles, farmers were shooting themselves in the foot. Eagles had feasted on the few sheep that died of cold or wild dog attack. But they rarely, if ever, killed healthy sheep. Unfortunately, by the time farmers discovered that eagles weren't killing sheep, thousands of eagles had been shot.

Do Flies Come from Rancid Meat?

Many myths about animals are based on misunderstandings. Not so long ago, it was believed that maggots sprang from spoiled meat. People thought that if meat rotted long enough, maggots would grow out of it. No connection was made between the flies that crawled over rotting meat and the maggots that later appeared.

People once thought that salamanders were created by fire. What the people didn't know was that hollow logs make great hiding places for salamanders. When hollow logs were thrown onto a fire, salamanders fled from the flames. The people seeing that thought that the animals were created by the fire.

Other myths people once believed were that geese grew from barnacles and that certain snakes drank milk. And there was also the "fact" that mice sprang to life from old shirt boxes.

A Goose from a Barnacle?

In northern Europe during the 13th century, there was a strange belief. People thought that a type of goose

barnacle: A small sea creature with a hard shell.

grew from barnacles—like a frog grows from a tadpole! This goose is still called the barnacle goose. The barnacles from which it was supposed to grow are called goose barnacles.

This story arose—like so many other myths—from a desire to explain the unknown. In this case, people wondered about the sudden appearance of the geese every autumn. In fact, the geese had flown from the Russian grasslands where they bred.

A Snake That Drinks Milk from a Cow?

Milk snakes are a group of brightly-banded nonpoisonous snakes from Central and North America. The milk snakes are so-named because of a strange story—that they drink milk directly from a cow! Actually, milk snakes mostly eat small rodents. They do not drink milk from cows or any other mammals.

Why Are Myths Sometimes Dangerous?

These stories seem funny to us today. There is no need to change the names of the barnacle goose or the milk snake simply because they are based on myths. These names add color to the language. However, myths can lead to killing animals as

pests. So, it is important to
know scientific facts.

In the Middle Ages,
cats were strongly
linked with evil and
witchcraft. Many cats
were treated cruelly.
For example, some
were put in boxes and
burned on bonfires.
Today we know that cats have no special powers.

Until quite recently, gorillas of Central and West
Africa were seen as savage King Kongs. They were
thought to roar and chest-beat their way through
the rain forest. Sometimes gorillas act this way.
But that is the gorilla's way of protecting its
territory from invaders. Closer studies of gorillas
showed them to be peaceful animals. They
actually spend most of their time eating leaves.

In fairy tales, the wolf is usually a mean killer.
Think of the story of *Little Red Riding Hood*. The
wolf tried to eat the little girl by pretending to be
the girl's grandmother. Even the coyote, a relative
of the wolf, is cast as the bad guy in cartoons.

Actually there are very few cases of wolves
killing people. Yet this animal is still hunted as a
killer.

Monsters of the Imagination

The human imagination is a powerful force. It shapes how we see the world. Have you ever been startled by a noise at night and imagined that there was danger there? You picture a monster lurking in the dark. Then you discover it was just a bush swaying in the breeze or a coat hanging on a door. People want explanations for what they see or hear. When what they observe is incomplete, imagination fills in the gaps.

Sea Monsters and Mermaids

Centuries ago, crews of sailing ships probably saw many animals they didn't recognize. From the deck of a ship, a walrus with only its head and shoulders above water might have looked like a sea person. Maybe the story of the mermaid—a half-woman, half-fish creature—started from the

sight of a walrus sitting upright in the sea. When it dived, it would have shown its fish-like tail.

Human imagination fills in what people don't understand. Imagination and time make mythical creatures real.

Is There a Loch Ness Monster?

Like Bigfoot, the Loch Ness Monster is a mythical creature many people believe exists.

St. Columba was the first person to report seeing the Loch Ness Monster. According to the story. St. Columba's brother was swimming in Loch Ness—a long and very deep lake in Scotland. Suddenly a monster appeared. The monster moved in to attack his brother. St. Columba shouted, "Go back," and so saved his brother's life. The monster must have been very shy, but its legend grew.

In 1933, a man driving around Loch Ness said he saw a strange animal about a mile offshore. He stopped his car to investigate. The man described the animal as he saw it from that distance. It was about 30 feet long with two humps. It had a snake-like head at the end of a long neck and two flippers near the middle of the body. Two local people also reported seeing something that resembled a whale.

The next year, in 1934, a photograph of a head and neck coming out of the water added to the excitement. The photograph was later found to be a fake.

Scientists have studied Loch Ness. Deep-sea divers have explored the lake too. But, there is still no proof that the Loch Ness Monster exists, or ever did.

Many of the people who live near Loch Ness rely on tourists for their income. So they do not try to disprove the myth. If the story were disproved, these people would lose the money the tourist trade brings. A mystery is much more profitable.

Besides, there's nothing wrong with a little mystery in the world, is there?

Are Owls Really Wise?

Humans see the world in terms of their own experience. We think owls are wise because their eyes are large and their heads turn slowly as they look at us. These human-like qualities make us think of someone with great wisdom. In the same way, lions are thought to be noble. They are called the king of beasts because of their size, strength, and seeming fearlessness.

Of course, owls and lions represent *positive* human qualities. People respect the qualities of wisdom and nobility. So people respect these animals.

Other animals represent *negative* human traits. We think foxes are cunning. Snakes are evil. Pigs are gluttons. And monkeys are tricksters.

Giving human traits to animals can lead us to misunderstand the world. The supposed slyness of the fox has helped to justify fox hunting. Is the fox really sly? When you see a fox in the wild, the fox stares at you for a moment. Then it quickly disappears into the countryside. At that moment a fox may appear sly. The truth is, to a fox, you are a danger to be avoided.

Indian Wolf: Misunderstood?

Of all the wolves in the world, the Indian wolf is the most rare. There are probably only 1,000 left in northern India. Farmers who live near the Indian wolf believe the wolf is to blame for their loss of cattle and sheep. Because of this, the Indian wolf is hunted down.

Scientists are currently studying Indian wolves to see whether the farmers are right. It may be that wild dogs are the real killers. If they are, maybe the Indian wolf will survive.

What Are Aesop's Fables?

Aesop is said to have been a Greek slave who lived in the Middle East sometime between 620 and 560 B.C. Aesop wrote many fables—stories that have a moral or a message. This collection of stories is known as Aesop's Fables. The fables use animals acting like humans to make a point.

The Fable of the Fox and the Crow

A crow, perched in a tree, held a piece of cheese that it had snatched from the ground. A hungry fox, seeing the cheese in the crow's beak, began to speak.

"Crow, you are beautiful. Surely your voice must be the most beautiful of all birds."

At this, the crow opened her beak and began to caw her best. Of course, the cheese fell from her mouth to the ground. The crow continued to caw as the fox took off with his prize.

In this fable, the fox is cast as crafty and sly. The crow represents stupidity or vanity. The moral of the story is "Watch out for sweet-talkers."

Finally . . .

There are an estimated 30 million animal species in the world. Of these, scientists have studied and named only 1.5 million. These are the animals we see every day in our neighborhoods, on TV, or when we visit a zoo.

This book has described just some examples of what people think about animals. It is not easy to explain why people treat animals a certain way. Or why they think of certain animals as they do.

Perhaps this is a question for each person to answer. What about you?

Where to from Here?

You've just read facts about the way we share our world with animals and interact with them. Here are some ideas for finding out more about human-animal relationships.

The Library

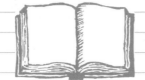

Some books you might enjoy include:
- *To the Top of the World: Adventures with Arctic Wolves*, by Jim Brandenburg
- *In the Company of Whales*, by Alexandra Morton
- *The Call of the Wolves*, by Jim Murphy
- *Wildlife Rescue, the Work of Dr. Kathleen Ramsay*, by Jennifer Owings Dewey

TV, Film, and Video

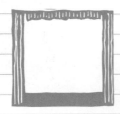

Watch TV listings for Public Broadcasting Station (PBS) programs and National Geographic specials about animals.
Visit a video store or your library to find films about people interacting with animals.

The Internet

There is a wealth of information about nature and animals on the Internet. Start with such key words as *animal attacks* and *endangered animals*. Also enter the names of specific animals you want to learn about.

People and Places

You might try your local 4-H Club, which educates young people about domestic animals. Many zoos have educational resources about animals that are native to other countries.

The Ultimate Fiction Book

Be sure to check out *Wolf Cry*, the companion volume to *Animal Attack*. *Wolf Cry* tells the story of a boy lost deep in the jungle in India who is adopted by a wolf family.

Decide for yourself where fact stops and fiction begins.

Index